AF580300

BY Celeste Mohammed ILLUSTRATED BY Cory Thomas

SPREE

The Boy Who Made the Steelpan Sing

GREENWILLOW BOOKS
An Imprint of HarperCollins*Publishers*

A long time ago, on the Caribbean island of Trinidad, there lived a boy named Winston. He was always asking questions, always running off to see what was going on, always having fun. People called him "Spree."

Spree's family was poor and, being the youngest boy, he didn't have much of anything to call his own. He watched his older brothers and sisters give up school and go into the city to find work. That would be his fate, too, he guessed.

But one day, Spree's father called them together and said, "Children, things ain't too bright here in Rose Hill. We moving to John-John. Plenty factories over there, so we'll find better work."

Spree was sad. He didn't want to leave his friends or his beloved mango tree, where the yellow-and-black birds would gather and sing, "Kis-ka-dee!" But his favorite brother, Joseph, lived in John-John already. So Spree perked up. *I wonder what it would be like over there?* he asked himself.

Whoa! John-John turned out to be exciting and full of life. A biscuit factory, a soap factory, a candle factory . . . so many places, with workers passing by every day. Spree woke up to the sh-sh-sh-shuffling of their feet and the whirr-rr-ing of their bicycles down the road.

John-John was loud! The clang-clanging of the railway repair yard and the whoot-whooting of factory whistles marked the times of each day. Spree got used to the mule-and-cart clackety-clacking and the trucks vroom-vrooming as they delivered stuff and took stuff away. Spree liked to stand at the roadside, eyes wide, ears twitching, mind curious about everything.

John-John was a messy place, too. Garbage from the factories spilled everywhere—tins and bins, pans and shipping drums, buckets and bowls, wooden sticks and rubber strips, scraps of metal.

Spree poked and prodded through the junk, turning things over with his foot.

"Look at this!" he'd shout, holding up something bent, broken, or shiny. Possibilities were everywhere.

That's how Spree discovered that John-John could be a musical place, too.

"Where you going, Joe?" he asked every Friday evening when Joe returned from work.

"By the corner to lime," his brother said.

With no money for fancy places, Joe and his friends limed on street corners. They talked, laughed, and sang about the things that made them happy and the things that made them sad.

"I could come? Please, please, please?" Spree asked every time.

"If you behave yourself," Joe answered one day. "Here, carry the drum."

What an honor! To carry Joe's cherished kettledrum—an old biscuit tin—dented and not so shiny anymore, but full of sound.

As Joe and his friends sang, somebody started clapping (clap, clap, clap!), then somebody added foot-stomping (duff, duff, duff!), somebody knocked a bottle and spoon (likki-ting, likki-ting, likki-ting!), somebody clanged two pieces of iron (tang-ta-tang!), somebody tapped a length of bamboo (tock, tock, tock!), and Joe slapped his kettledrum (da-da-da-DUM).

Spree closed his eyes and let the rhythm carry him clear above the clutter of John-John.

Up, up . . . like a bird on the wing.

CRAX
CRACKERS

Spree danced for joy on the day he got his own drum. A biscuit tin, like his brother's, but with a special sound from its lighter, softer metal.

Now Spree watched Joe even more closely when he drummed. He tried to copy each beat, each slap, each roll. At first his hands got swollen—they stung for days—but Spree didn't mind. He wanted to play better than Joe. He wanted to be the best drummer in John-John!

When he was beating that drum, Spree felt there was something inside him fluttering and pecking its way out, trying to make itself melodious and free.

Soon enough, Spree became the leader of his own John-John rhythm band. Their happiest times were Carnival days, when everyone from all over Trinidad took to the big city to dance, sing, and parade through the streets.

But then World War II began. The city went quiet. No more Carnival. No more parades. Factories closed, jobs disappeared, food grew scarce. Everyone was scared.

Did that stop Spree and the people of John-John? Not for long! They held secret sing-alongs and little parades, not in the big city but through their own narrow lanes. Sometimes, the police caught them. A few of Spree's friends even went to jail. But they kept at it. Rhythm was how they shook off their fear.

Then one day, after parading through the neighborhood and beating his drum till his hands hummed, Spree longed to "leh go" like the carefree spectators. To prance and dance, to wave and shake, to get caught up in the rhythm of the other drums.

"Go ahead. I'll hold yours," his friend Shaker, a big strong guy, said.

So Spree handed over his drum.

He returned to find that his beloved pan had been drummed by Shaker until it was now . . . a bowl? The special tone of Spree's drum was gone!

Spree ran home, grabbed a rock from the yard, and began pounding the inside of his drum, trying to fix it. At first, he pounded with all his might. Then, when the rock hurt his hand, he switched to a piece of wood, pounding slower now, tired, but still trying to remove the dents.

Ping! A strange clear note rang out. Spree froze, then smiled. Time to experiment. He hit the pan again in a different spot. Pong! He tried another dent. Ping! Then another. Pong! By tapping the wooden stick on different dents, with different strengths, he'd made four different sounds, almost like real musical notes.

This was new! This was exciting! This was beyond rhythm!

This was . . . melody!

"Joe, come quick!" Spree said when his brother arrived home. "My pan can sing!"

Joe crouched beside him, listening. His eyes widened.

"Is true!" he whispered to Spree. "The thing singing!"

Joe shook his head in awe. "I heard some fellas been trying to do this, but I didn't think it could work."

"Who?" Spree demanded. "Where? How do they do it? I need to meet them!"

Spree spent the rest of the war years searching for anyone who could teach him how to find more melody inside his old steel pan. He asked questions and watched the older panmen.

He pounded and tuned, hammered and tested. Night after night, by candle or flambeau, he tapped and listened. One note, then two, then three. Each one clearer than the last.

The music inside Spree's pan was waking up.

Then, at last, peace came. The island of Trinidad was dancing in the open again and looking forward to its first official Carnival in many years. But no one was more excited than sixteen-year-old Spree. He had a secret to share with everyone.

On Carnival Tuesday, 1946, he led his band through the city, then stepped alone onto the big downtown stage. His hands trembled. Would he make a mistake? Would he play it right? What if no one heard what he heard?

GOVERNOR

Through beads of sweat, Spree glimpsed the governor and other important folks in the stands. He shut his eyes and whispered, “Spree, boy, just believe.”

He pictured all the days he’d spent in the churchyard, under his favorite mango tree, listening to the melodies of hymns, the rustling of leaves, and the warbling of nature against the beat of the neighborhood. He saw all those nights he’d stayed awake by flickering flame, figuring out the notes of calypso songs. His arms twitched and tingled as they remembered the years and years of pounding. He took a deep breath.

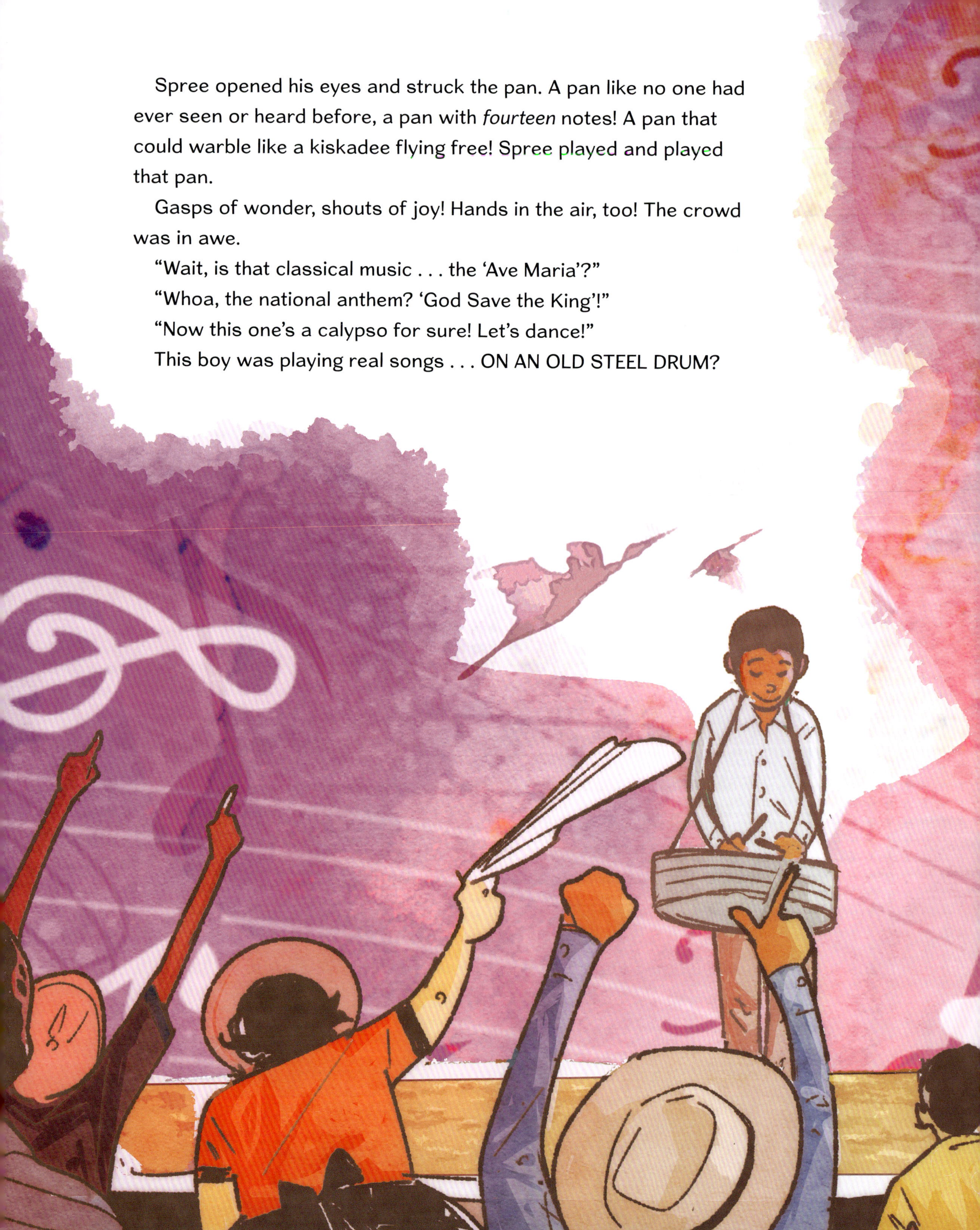

Spree opened his eyes and struck the pan. A pan like no one had ever seen or heard before, a pan with *fourteen* notes! A pan that could warble like a kiskadee flying free! Spree played and played that pan.

Gasps of wonder, shouts of joy! Hands in the air, too! The crowd was in awe.

"Wait, is that classical music . . . the 'Ave Maria'?"

"Whoa, the national anthem? 'God Save the King'!"

"Now this one's a calypso for sure! Let's dance!"

This boy was playing real songs . . . ON AN OLD STEEL DRUM?

“Hooray, hurrah!” the people cheered. Their own Spree had shown the world a thrilling new musical instrument. He’d proven that sweet melody can rise from anywhere—from a tiny yard in John-John, from the garbage and castoffs of a city, even from the hands of a curious boy with nothing much to call his own.

Yes, Spree had proven that there is music inside us all. You just need to listen for it.

Ping, pong, ping, pong. . . .

A NOTE ABOUT THE STEELPAN

The steelpan is the national instrument of the Caribbean island nation of Trinidad and Tobago. It is considered the only acoustic instrument invented in the twentieth century. Nowadays, steelpan orchestras can be found throughout Europe, North America, and as far as Asia. However, the instrument had its humble beginnings during the 1930s and '40s, in the ghettos of Trinidad's capital city, Port of Spain.

Winston "Spree" Simon in 1953. Photo by Larry Keighley for the Saturday Evening Post. *Courtesy of Pan Trinbago Inc.*

The white upper class of Trinidad plantation society had always celebrated Carnival. In the olden days—during the 1700s and 1800s—they crowded into pretty ballrooms for masquerade balls with fine musicians and, much later, gramophones. Meanwhile, the plantation slaves created their own version of the festival. They mimicked their masters' fancy dress and made music with whatever was at hand—animal-skin drums, lengths of bamboo, pieces of metal from the stables, and so on.

After slavery ended, Black people took their Carnival parades onto the streets. In the early twentieth century, many crowded into Port of Spain, looking for work. Depressed working-class areas, like Rose Hill and John-John, sprang up on the outskirts of the city. At this time, African drumming—as their ancestors had done on the plantations—was outlawed. The people adjusted yet again by making rhythm with whatever was at hand, including the garbage of the city's factories, such as dustbins, biscuit tins, and the empty oil drums that were plentiful due to Trinidad's vibrant oil industry.

Somewhere around the 1930s, an accidental discovery was made: when dented, the sound of metal containers changed. Young Black men, like Spree, pushed that discovery to its limit. With barely any education and no formal music training, they became inventors—hammering, stretching, and tuning the surfaces of metal drums, searching for harmonic sound. They obsessed over their craft, and soon enough, the first "ping-pong" pans appeared, some with only three notes but able to carry a simple melody. Within a few years, every ghetto in Port of Spain had its own steelpan orchestra.

While no single person can be credited with inventing the steelpan, it is agreed that sixteen-year-old Spree Simon (1930–1976) was the boy genius who first made the world aware of steelpan's potential as a musical instrument. On Carnival Tuesday in 1946, he unveiled a fourteen-note steelpan and played, among other things, Schubert's "Ave Maria" and "God Save the King," becoming the first person to demonstrate to the world the melodic potential of steelpan.

No one had ever before produced that level of music from industrial waste.

Spree remained a panman for the rest of his life. He was the leader of several steel bands. He was a mentor, freely sharing his knowledge with aspiring pan tuners. He was a goodwill ambassador of the pan, taking this unique music to various parts of the world.

Spree died in 1976, but his contribution as a pioneer of steelpan has not been forgotten. A statue of him exists in my hometown, San Fernando, Trinidad, and several songs have been written about him. The most famous one goes like this:

Everybody wond'ring of how the steel band start.
You like to know?
When you get to know, well,
it's gonna break your heart.
I tell you now, it's founded by one Winston Spree.
This is how he started his first melody.

—"Tribute to Spree Simon" by Lord Kitchener (1975)

Want to make your own rhythm? Grab a spoon and a pot—or two sticks and a bucket. Close your eyes. Start tapping. Listen close. Like Spree, you just might hear something new.

Discover More About the Steelpan

A Brief History of Steelpan—
Chicago Youth Symphony Orchestras: www.youtube.com/watch?v=rJEjVR4gtgU
The history of steelpan, as told by students from CYSO's steel orchestras.
For more information on Chicago Youth Symphony Orchestras' steelpan programs, visit: www.cyso.org/orchestras/steel-orchestras.

Turning Nothing into Something: The History of the Steel Pan—
CBC Arts: www.youtube.com/watch?v=XMWksr7oS4A
Jaigan McKenley-McDonald shares the history of steelpan—where it originated, why it is the sound of Carnival, and how it connects him to his own Trinidadian heritage.

Making a Steelpan—
Brainbuilders_tutoring: www.youtube.com/watch?v=INRyc5WZqRc
This video guides kids and parents through the process of creating a steelpan together. The video provides step-by-step instructions using readily available materials, including a tin can, hammer, and bamboo. The creator also shares the history of the steelpan, highlighting its origins in Trinidad and Tobago and the key figures who shaped its development.

Sounds Like Steel, directed by Chas Sheppard: www.youtube.com/watch?v=SGJQ0_BLMGI
Though not kid-specific, this is a great documentary about the national instrument of Trinidad and Tobago.

Alkins, Jeunanne. *Play ah Mas*. With contributions by Keron Boodoosingh, Nicolas Huggins, and Adira Khan. Everything Slight Paper, 2024.
For readers who want to learn more about the traditional Masquerade (Mas) characters of Trinidad Carnival, this book is a fun resource.

If you're ever in Trinidad, you can visit Musical Instruments of Trinidad and Tobago Company Limited (MITTCO) for a tour, where you can witness the step-by-step process of converting a steel drum into a steelpan instrument.
Visit online: www.mittcott.com.

To Sarai, Miguel, Elevyn, and Caleb—
May you always remember that
greatness can grow on small islands
—C. M.

For my home.
—C. T.

HarperCollins Children's Books, a division of HarperCollins Publishers,
195 Broadway, New York, NY 10007

HarperCollins Publishers, Macken House, 39/40 Mayor Street Upper,
Dublin 1, D01 C9W8, Ireland

Greenwillow Books is an imprint of HarperCollins Publishers.

Spree: The Boy Who Made the Steelpan Sing

harpercollins.com

ISBN 978-0-06-309324-9

The illustrations in this book combine digital line art, painting techniques, and graphic elements.
The text of this book is set in 13-point Cardigan. Book design by Paul Zakris.
26 27 28 29 30 RTLO 10 9 8 7 6 5 4 3 2 1
First Edition

Greenwillow Books